THE STATES AND THEIR SYMBOLS

Ohio
Facts and Symbols

by Emily McAuliffe

Consultant:
Sandra Miller
Ohio Department of Education
Division of Early Childhood Education

Hilltop Books
an imprint of Franklin Watts
A Division of Grolier Publishing
New York   London   Hong Kong   Sydney
Danbury, Connecticut

Hilltop Books
http://publishing.grolier.com

Library of Congress Cataloging-in-Publication Data
McAuliffe, Emily.
  Ohio facts and symbols/by Emily McAuliffe.
    p. cm.—(The states and their symbols)
  Includes bibliographical references and index.
  Summary: Presents information about the state of Ohio and its nickname, motto,
and emblems.
  ISBN 0-7368-0085-9
  1. Emblems, State—Ohio—Juvenile literature. [1. Emblems, State—Ohio. 2. Ohio.]
I. Title. II. Series: McAuliffe, Emily. States and their symbols.
CR203.O3M38 1999
977.1—DC21

                                                                    98-7359
                                                                        CIP
                                                                         AC

Editorial Credits
Michaela Van Deusen, editor; James Franklin, cover designer and illustrator; Sheri Gosewisch,
    photo researcher

Photo Credits
Capitol Square Review and Advisory Board, 10
Dembinsky Photo Assoc., Inc./Doug Locke, 20
Eastern National/Kelly Faris, 22 (bottom)
Ohio Historical Society/Tom Root, 22 (top)
One Mile Up, Inc., 8; 10 (inset)
Unicorn Stock Photography/Dede Gilman, cover; Ted Rose, 6; Richard B. Dippold, 12;
    Martha McBride, 14; A. Gurmankin, 16
United States Air Force Museum, 22 (middle)
Visuals Unlimited/William J. Weber, 18

Table of Contents

Fast Facts about Ohio

Capital: Columbus is the capital of Ohio.

Largest City: Columbus is the largest city in Ohio. More than 600,000 people live in Columbus.

Size: Ohio covers 44,828 square miles (116,105 square kilometers).

Location: Ohio is in the midwestern United States. It is one of the Great Lakes states.

Population: Ohio is home to 11,186,331 people (U.S. Census Bureau, 1997 estimate).

Statehood: Ohio became the 17th state on March 1, 1803.

Natural Resources: Ohio companies mine coal and limestone. They also mine sand, gravel, and salt.

Manufactured Goods: Factories in Ohio make iron, steel, and soap. They also make rubber tires, hoses, and rubber bands.

Crops: Ohio farmers grow soybeans, corn, and winter wheat. They also raise dairy cows.

State Name and Nickname

Ohio means large or beautiful in the Iroquois (EAR-uh-kwoi) language. The Iroquois are a group of Native Americans. The Iroquois gave this name to the Ohio River. Early settlers in the area named the land Ohio too.

Ohio's official nickname is the Buckeye State. This nickname comes from the buckeye tree. This tree once grew in all areas of Ohio. Early settlers used buckeye wood to build their homes.

The Iroquois gave the buckeye tree its name. They thought the buckeye seed looked like a buck's eye. A buck is a male deer.

The Mother of Modern Presidents is another nickname for Ohio. Seven former U.S. presidents were born in the state. William McKinley was the last president born in Ohio. He became the 25th president of the United States in 1897.

The Iroquois thought the buckeye seed looked like a buck's eye.

State Seal and Motto

Ohio adopted its original state seal in 1803. The state seal is a symbol. It reminds Ohioans of their state's government. The seal also makes government papers official.

Ohio changed its seal in 1996. The current seal shows a rising sun with 13 rays. These rays stand for the country's original 13 states. Wheat honors Ohio's farmers. The seal also has a nature scene. It honors the state's rivers, mountains, and valleys.

The seal also shows a grouping of 17 arrows. These arrows stand for Ohio's state ranking. Ohio was the 17th state to join the United States.

Ohio has an official state motto. A motto is a word or saying that people believe in. Ohio's motto is "With God, all things are possible." This sentence comes from the Bible. Ohio's government made the sentence the state motto in 1959.

Ohio adopted its state seal in 1803.

State Capitol and Flag

The state capitol building is in Columbus. Columbus is Ohio's capital city. Government officials work in the capitol. They meet there to make the state's laws.

Ohio has had three different capital cities. Its first capital was the city of Chillicothe. The government moved the capital to Zanesville in 1809. Officials voted to move the capital to Columbus in 1816. They wanted the capital to be in central Ohio.

Ohio's government approved plans for the current capitol building in 1838. Builders began work on the capitol the next year. They finished the capitol in 1861. Workers built the new capitol with Ohio stone.

Ohio's flag is different from other states' flags. Ohio's flag is a burgee. A burgee is a narrow, triangle-shaped flag. Ohio adopted its flag in 1902.

The state capitol building is in Columbus.

State Bird

The cardinal became Ohio's state bird in 1933. The cardinal lives throughout Ohio.

Male and female cardinals have crests. A crest is a tuft of feathers on a bird's head. Cardinals are easy birds to recognize because of these crests.

Adult cardinals measure about nine inches (23 centimeters) in length. Males have bright red feathers. They also have black markings around their faces and throats. Female cardinals have brown feathers. Their crests, wing tips, and tails are red-brown.

Cardinals build their nests in shrubs and bushes. They make nests out of twigs and leaves. Cardinals build their nests in the shape of a cup. Females lay three or four eggs at one time. These eggs are pale green with dark spots.

Male and female cardinals have crests.

State Tree

The buckeye became Ohio's state tree in 1953. Buckeye trees are native to some midwestern states.

Buckeyes can grow to be 50 feet (15 meters) tall. These trees grow best near rivers and lakes. Young buckeye trees have light brown bark. The bark of older trees is rough and dark brown.

The buckeye has broad, flat leaves. Each leaf has a stem with five smaller leaves attached. These leaves have rough, uneven edges.

The seeds of the buckeye tree have thick outer shells. The round, shiny seeds are dark brown with tan spots. Squirrels eat buckeye seeds. But the seeds will make humans ill.

Some people carry buckeye seeds in their pockets for good luck. This practice comes from an old belief. This belief said people who carried buckeyes would come into money.

The buckeye became Ohio's state tree in 1953.

State Flower

The scarlet carnation became Ohio's state flower in 1904. The government chose this flower in honor of President McKinley.

President McKinley believed the scarlet carnation brought him good luck. He always wore a scarlet carnation on his lapel. A lapel is the fold of the front of a coat. President McKinley also kept an arrangement of carnations on his desk. He would give one carnation to each White House guest.

Carnations once grew only in the wild. Gardeners now raise these flowers in greenhouses. A greenhouse is a warm building where plants can grow year-round.

Carnations live a long time after they are picked. Carnations also have a pleasant scent. Florists use carnations in flower arrangements for these reasons.

The scarlet carnation became Ohio's state flower in 1904.

State Animal

The white-tailed deer became Ohio's state animal in 1988. Many white-tailed deer live in the hills of eastern Ohio.

White-tailed deer have red-brown fur during summer. Their coats turn gray when the weather becomes cold. The deer have white chests and stomachs.

White-tailed deer also have bushy, white tails. The deer raise their tails when they sense danger. This warns other deer that danger may be near.

Female deer are called does. Newborn deer are called fawns. Fawns are born in May or June with white spots on their red-brown fur. The spots fade when fawns are a few months old.

Deer rest during the day and feed in the evening. They eat soft bark, twigs, and leaves from trees. White-tailed deer also eat grasses and shrub leaves.

A fawn is born with white spots on its red-brown fur.

More State Symbols

State Wildflower: Ohio adopted the trillium as the state wildflower in 1987. Each trillium has three large, white petals. These petals turn pink as the flower ages.

State Gem: Ohio flint became the official gem in 1965. Flint is a hard, gray stone. People usually dig up flint in quarries.

State Insect: The ladybug is Ohio's state insect. Ohio school children chose the ladybug in 1975.

State Song: "Beautiful Ohio" became Ohio's state song in 1969. Ballard MacDonald wrote this song about the Ohio River.

State Rock Song: Ohio also has an official rock song. "Hang On Sloopy" became Ohio's state rock song in 1985. A band called The McCoys first recorded this hit song. This band was from Dayton, Ohio.

Each trillium has three large, white petals.

Places to Visit

Serpent Mound

Native Americans built the Serpent Mound more than 2,000 years ago. This mound is an ancient burial ground. Native Americans shaped the mound like a giant snake. The best view of the mound is from the air. The Serpent Mound is near the town of Peebles in Adams County, Ohio.

United States Air Force Museum

The United States Air Force Museum is in Dayton, Ohio. This museum contains more than 300 types of aircraft. For example, visitors can see a Curtiss P-40E Warhawk. U.S. Army Air Forces used this plane in World War II (1939-1945).

Perry's Victory and International Peace Memorial

Perry's Victory and International Peace Memorial is on South Bass Island in Lake Erie. It is near the town of Put-in-Bay. The memorial honors Commodore Oliver Perry. Perry led the U.S. Navy to victory in the Battle of Lake Erie. This battle took place during the War of 1812 (1812-1814).

Words to Know

burgee (BUR-gee)—a narrow, triangle-shaped flag
crest (KREST)—a tuft of feathers on a bird's head
greenhouse (GREEN-houss)—a warm building where plants can grow year-round
lapel (luh-PEL)—the fold of the front of a coat
quarry (KWOR-ee)—a place where people dig up stone
symbol (SIM-buhl)—something that stands for or suggests something else; the U.S. flag is a symbol of the United States.

Read More

Brown, Dottie. *Ohio.* Hello USA. Minneapolis: Lerner Publications, 1993.

Capstone Press Geography Dept. *Ohio.* One Nation. Mankato, Minn.: Capstone Press, 1996.

Fradin, Dennis B. *Ohio.* From Sea to Shining Sea. Chicago: Children's Press, 1993.

Thompson, Kathleen. *Ohio.* Portrait of America. Austin, Texas: Raintree Steck-Vaughn, 1996.

Useful Addresses

**Office of the Ohio
    Secretary of State**
30 East Broad Street
Columbus, OH 43215

Ohio State Library
65 South Front Street
Columbus, OH 43215

Internet Sites

OH! Kids—Stuff to Do
http://www.oplin.lib.oh.us/EDUCATE/STUFF
Ohio Citizen's Digest
http://www.oplin.lib.oh.us/OHIO/OCJ/index.html
Ohio Historical Society Kids' Pages
http://www.ohiohistory.org/kids

Index